# SWEET SUGAR

Written by
John Wood

Enslow
PUBLISHING

Published in 2022 by Enslow Publishing, LLC
29 East 21st Street, New York, NY 10010

Copyright © 2021 Booklife Publishing
This edition published by arrangement with Booklife Publishing

Cataloging-in-Publication Data

Names: Wood, John, 1990-.
Title: Sweet sugar / John Wood.
Description: New York : Enslow Publishing, 2022. | Series: Brain food | Includes glossary and index.
Identifiers: ISBN 9781978523807 (pbk.) | ISBN 9781978523821 (library bound) | ISBN 9781978523814 (6 pack) |
ISBN 9781978523838 (ebook)
Subjects: LCSH: Sugars in human nutrition--Juvenile literature. | Nutrition--Juvenile literature.
Classification: LCC TX553.S8 W66 2022 | DDC 641.3'08--dc23

Designer: Jasmine Pointer
Editor: William Anthony

Printed in the United States of America

CPSIA compliance information: Batch #CSENS22: For further information contact Enslow Publishing, New York, New York at 1-800-398-2504

Find us on  

# PHOTO CREDITS

# CONTENTS

Words that look like <u>this</u> can be found in the glossary on page 24.

# A SLICE OF SCIENCE

Did your mom tell you not to eat chocolate for breakfast? Do adults keep trying to feed you bananas? You might be wondering: why does it matter what I eat?

Hello! I'm a small scientist. I'm here to teach you about food. Food is very important!

You might have heard the words "healthy diet." A diet is the kinds of food you usually eat. To have a healthy diet, you need to make sure you eat many different kinds of food.

A healthy diet is often called a balanced diet because you eat lots of different types of food.

# PORTIONS

But how do we <u>measure</u> the amount of food? A portion, or serving, of food is the amount a person eats in one sitting.

Sometimes portions are measured in ounces. You can use a food scale like this one to weigh food!

A serving of food might be half a grapefruit.

Different foods have different portion sizes. You should have five servings of fruits and vegetables a day. A serving of fruit is roughly the amount you can fit in the palm of your hand.

# WHAT IS SUGAR?

There are two types of sugar: <u>natural</u> sugars and added sugars.

Sugar is something found in food. It gives you <u>energy</u>. But having too much sugar can be harmful to the body. That's why sweets should be just an occasional treat!

You probably know many of the sweet foods below! These examples all include added sugar.

Cookies

Candy

Muffins

Doughnuts

# LET'S EXPERIMENT!

We will need this mood bar. It will tell us about someone's body. It shows four things — how fast they are growing, <u>blood sugar</u> levels, how well they can concentrate, and how healthy their teeth are.

**GROWTH**

**BLOOD SUGAR**

**CONCENTRATION**

**TEETH**

GROWTH

BLOOD SUGAR

CONCENTRATION

TEETH

It is time to start the experiment. The mood bar is saying that this kid's teeth are not healthy. What shall we do?

# NOTHING BUT THE TOOTH

Here is the problem – too much soda, or pop! Sodas often have a lot of sugar in them. Too much sugar can <u>damage</u> teeth, so choosing to drink water instead of soda or juice most of the time is a good idea.

**Tooth <u>decay</u> can lead to teeth being taken out.**

Let's have a look at the next kid's mood bar. Her blood sugar levels are not normal. Let's find out what the problem is.

GROWTH

BLOOD SUGAR

CONCENTRATION

TEETH

13

# SNEAKY SUGAR

This child needs to add foods with protein, healthy fats, and carbohydrates to her diet! Eaten alone, sugary foods can cause blood sugar to go up and down quickly. It doesn't feel very good!

Ice cream is a nice treat!

Diabetes affects blood sugar levels, which can be dangerous.

**GROWTH**

**BLOOD SUGAR**

**CONCENTRATION**

**TEETH**

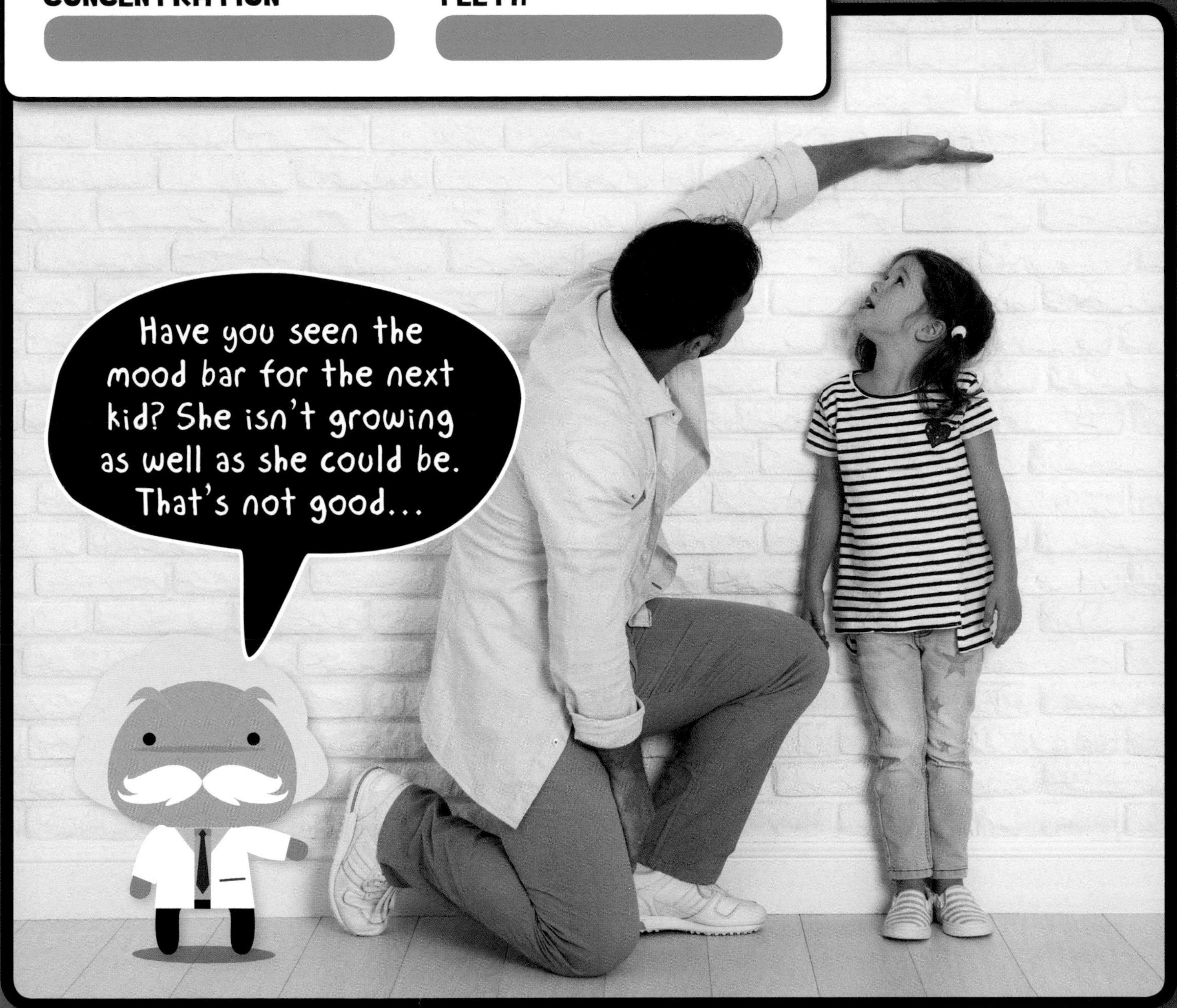

# SUGAR IN THE WAY

How about adding in some fruits and vegetables? Kids need <u>nutrients</u> to grow. Sugary foods like chocolate don't have many nutrients and shouldn't be the main part of your diet.

GROWTH

BLOOD SUGAR

CONCENTRATION

TEETH

Let's go to our last kid. The mood bar tells us she's finding it hard to concentrate. How can we help her?

# SUGAR BE GONE!

Let's swap cake for another breakfast choice, such as toast and eggs. Sugary foods give you quick energy. But this means you may get tired after that and find it harder to concentrate.

**Whole grain** cereal gives you good energy for your day.

The child is healthy and happy again. This experiment has gone quite well, don't you think?

**GROWTH**

**BLOOD SUGAR**

**CONCENTRATION**

**TEETH**

# FOOD SWAPS

Here are some ideas for snacks that will give you the nutrients you need and keep you full of energy all day long.

Cucumber sticks

Sugar-free Jell-O

**Mashed avocado**

**Yogurt with fruit**

**Boiled eggs**

**Whole wheat bread**

21

The examples below have added sugar in them. They're okay for an occasional treat!

Jell-O

Pudding

Dessert

Sugary cereals

# THE MOST IMPORTANT THING

Eating sugary foods can be yummy, but don't forget that you must eat lots of different types of food. This is what makes a diet healthy and balanced.

Carbs

Fruits and vegetables

Protein

Fats and sugars

low fat milk

Yogurt

Dairy

# GLOSSARY

| | |
|---|---|
| balanced | made up of the right or equal amounts |
| blood sugar | a type of sugar that is transported around the body in your blood |
| damage | to break or cause harm |
| diabetes | an illness in which the body has trouble controlling blood sugar levels, which can lead to damage to organs |
| energy | the ability to do something |
| measure | to find out the exact amount of something using units or systems, such as ounces for weight or feet for distance |
| natural | found in nature and not made by people |
| nutrients | things that plants and animals need to grow and stay healthy |
| tooth decay | when the outer layer of a tooth is destroyed or broken by bacteria |
| whole grain | containing the whole of the grain seed and all of the nutrients |

#  INDEX